INSTANT ART for BIBLE THEMES WORKSHEETS

Book Three

Compiled by
Susan Sayers

Illustrated by
Jennifer Carter

Kevin Mayhew

First published in 1995 in Great Britain by
KEVIN MAYHEW LTD
Rattlesden
Bury St Edmunds, Suffolk IP30 0SZ

Catalogue No 1396038
ISBN 0 86209 700 2

Cover by Sara Silcock
Typesetting by Vicky Brown
Printed in Great Britain

Contents

Alphabetical Index

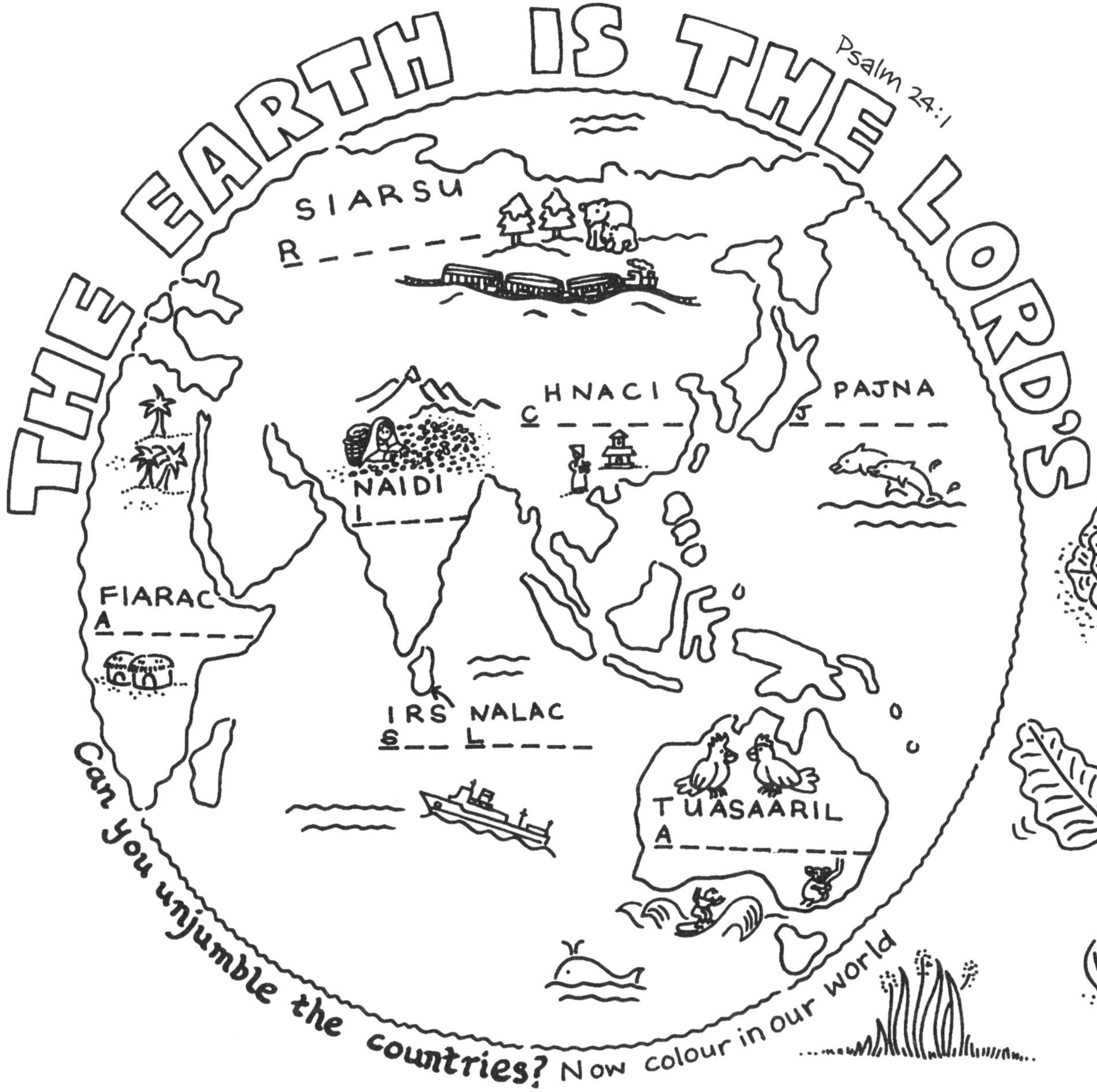

Draw a RED ring round the soft things.

Draw a GREEN ring round the green things.

Draw a BLUE ring round the things with 4 legs.

Draw a YELLOW ring round everything God made.

GOD is the one who made...

20,8,5 19,11,25

20,8,5 5,1,18,20,8

20,8,5 19,5,1

1,14,4 1,12,12 20,8,1,20 9,19 9,14, 20,8,5,13

Genesis 1

Colour these creatures and draw some of your own:

A	B	C	D	E	F	G	H	I	J	K	L	M	N	O	P	Q	R	S	T	U	V	W	X	Y	Z
1	2	3	4	5	6	7	8	9	10	11	12	13	14	15	16	17	18	19	20	21	22	23	24	25	26

GOD'S GLORY SHOWS

Do you know what GLORY means?

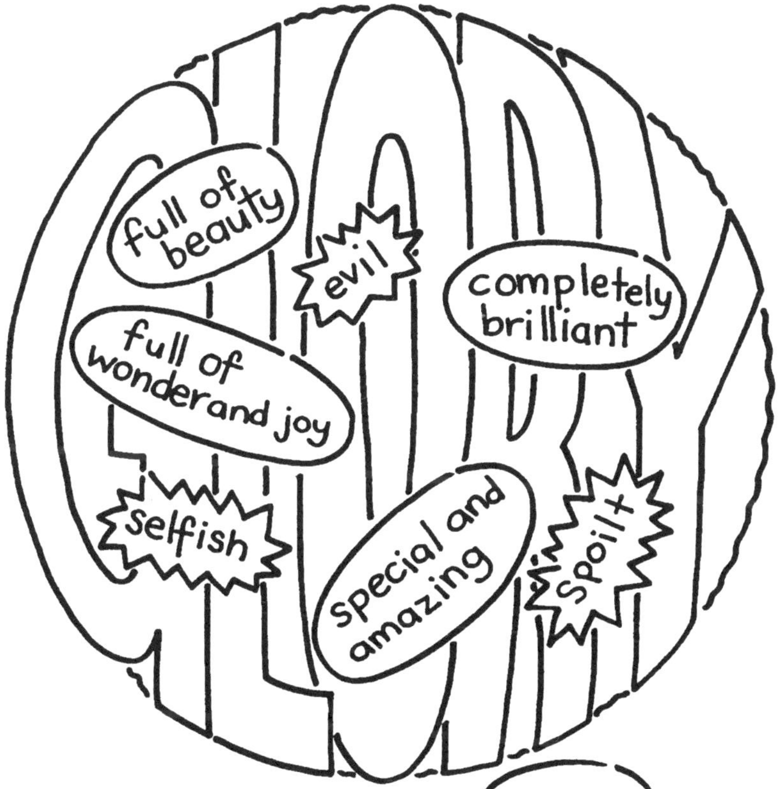

Colour in the 

Scribble out the 

Fill in the letters from the reflection:

God's glory is reflected in us.

WHEN?

whenever we are

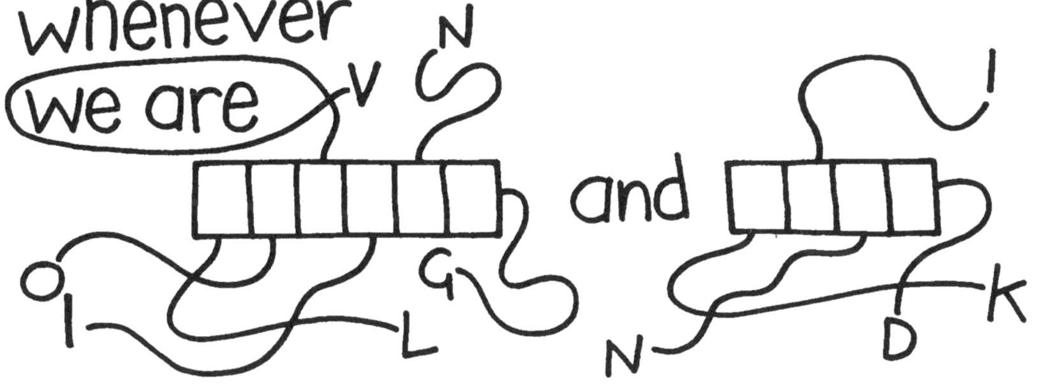

God is the one with real power.
THERE
WAS
ANYTHING
BEFORE
GOD
ELSE
Colour in your best colours
Mene
Mene
Tekel
Parsin
See if you can find out what these words mean? (Look at Daniel chapter 5 verses 25–28)
Which of these has most power?
God
people
The devil
Which of these has most light power?
Which of these has most heating power?

How does God think? What is he like?

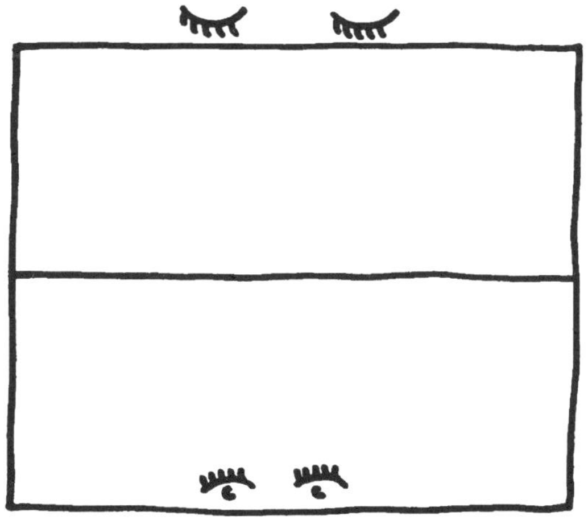

1. Close your eyes and try to draw an elephant.
2. Look at your picture. Now draw an elephant with your eyes open.

Which drawing is best?

Which is God's way?

HIDE AND SEEK. Can you spot 6 fish hidden in this picture?

Sometimes we have to seek for God before we find him.

What have you found out about God?

God is ______ I know, because ______

God is ______ I know, because ______

God is ______ I know, because ______

God is ______ I know, because ______

Who is the real GOD?

Put red circles round the true
Put blue squares around the false

God is generous

God picks on people

God does what you tell him to

God knows me and loves me

God knows what is best for me

God is pretend

God doesn't like to see me enjoying myself

God is alive and powerful

Here are some things that God made

Write here the names of some people you and God love.

G	O	D	A	E	G	I	J
M	C	F	B	D	J	K	E
C	H	R	I	S	T	L	S
L	O	R	D	P	U	A	U
O	L	H	N	I	V	Z	S
Q	Y	P	R	R	X	C	B
S	S	A	V	I	O	U	R
T	W	Y	D	T	E	H	L

Find 6 names of God.

God is in charge.

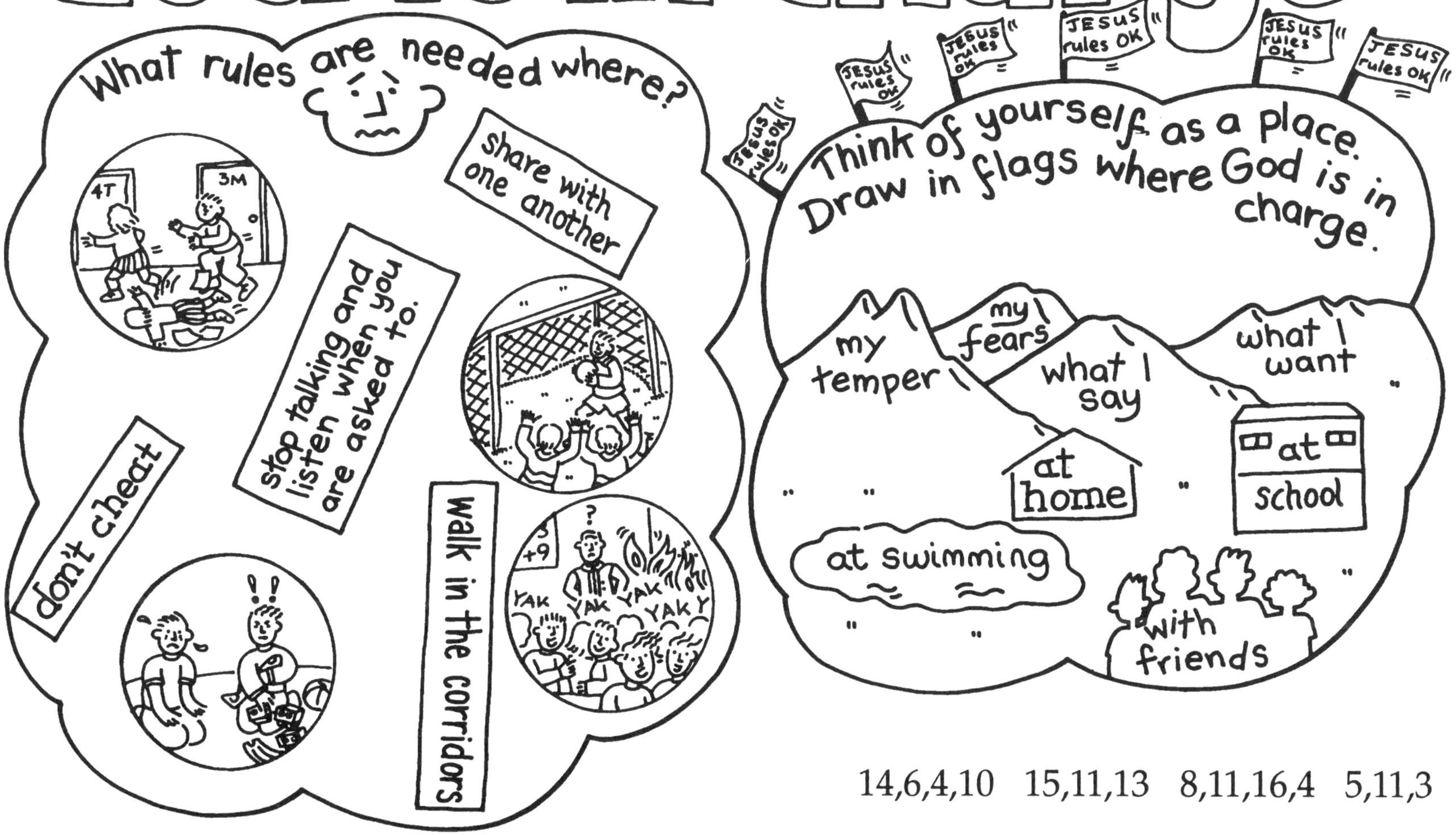

14,6,4,10 15,11,13 8,11,16,4 5,11,3

15,11,13 14,1,10,12 12,11 11,2,4,15 6,7,9

1,10,3 3,11 14,6,1,12 6,4 14,1,10,12,17.

A	B	D	E	G	H	I	L	M	N	O	T	U	W	Y	V	S
1	2	3	4	5	6	7	8	9	10	11	12	13	14	15	16	17

I AM GOD, THERE IS NO OTHER

Isaiah 46:9

When God decides to do something, he always does it. He decided to rescue us from sin and he did it. He wanted to save all of us, the whole human family, including you.

The word GENTILE means:~ AT PTERROSTOEN WIHTOR ILSH NOONTO JAELWHINSTHE (cross out every second letter)

Circle the odd ones out

Search for the message and colour it in.

God likes giving presents.

Here are some of them:

Which would you use to write with?

Which would you use to cut paper?

Which would you use to sew with?

Which are God's way, which are not?

being worried

being helpful

being greedy

being forgiving

being friendly

being mean

No present is any good unless—

.

God made us to live as he planned~  it works much better that way.

GOD'S LOVE COMES FREE OF CHARGE!

How much is the pen?	☐
How much is the drink?	☐
Does the pen cost the most?	☐
Is the balloon cheap?	☐
Can you buy 3 things for a £1?	☐
What does it cost to buy all the things?	☐
Is anything free?	☐

Most things cost money.
Some things are expensive.
God gives us his love.
It cost him his life.

Which of these things must you do to win God's love?

Draw some things you have had as presents and write underneath who gave them to you.

MARY SAID 'YES'

See Luke 1:26–38

Help the rescue team to reach the trapped man.

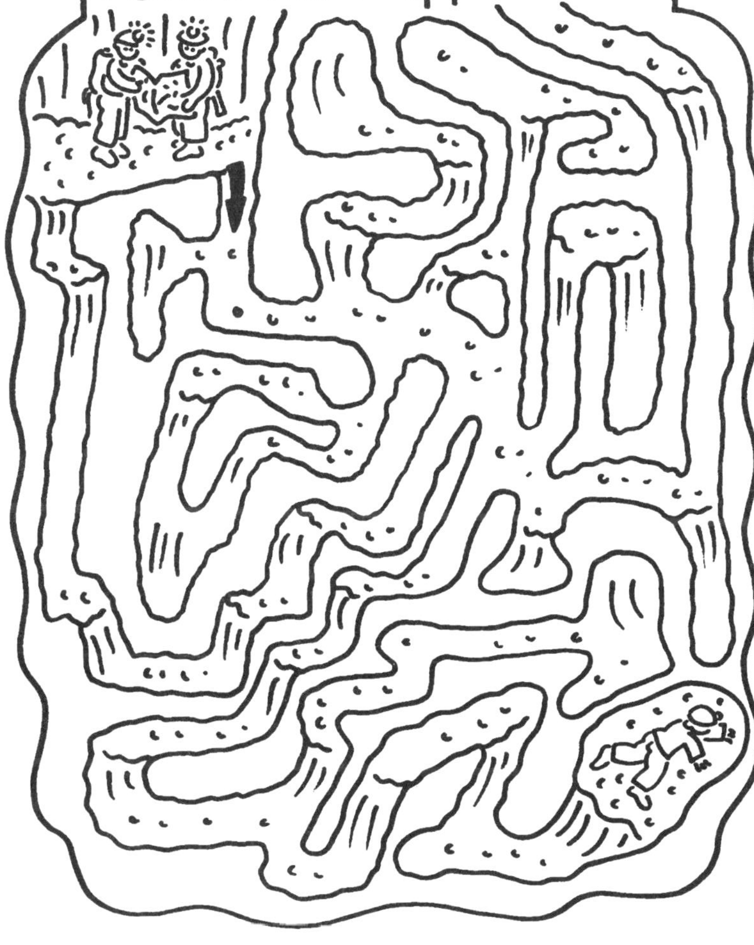

We were trapped in our SIN.

God had a RESCUE plan.

He would be born as a _ _ _ _ _ _ _ _ Y.

He would need a good, loving mother.

Who did God choose?

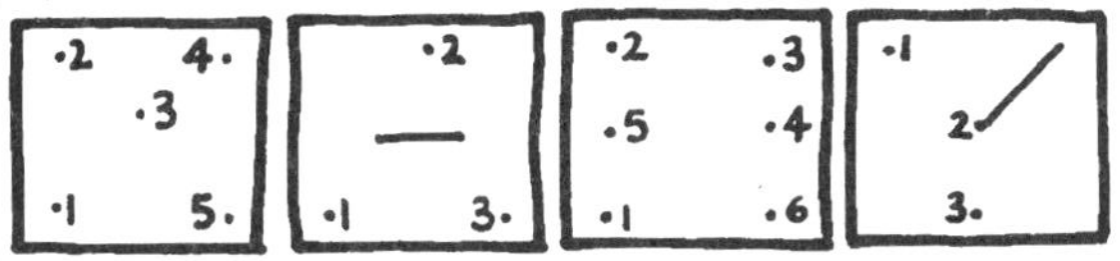

Who is in your family tree?

Draw them or write their names in here:

Q. Why is Jesus sometimes called the 'Son of David'?

A. Because Joseph (Mary's husband) was part of King David's family tree

JESUS IS BORN

Luke 2:1-20

M	A	H	F	N	U	R	V
A	J	W	M	E	A	O	B
R	C	O	B	T	L	T	S
Y	G	X	S	Q	L	K	T
D	O	N	K	E	Y	P	A
Q	I	I	G	D	P	A	B
Y	R	N	S	Z	J	H	L
M	A	N	G	E	R	C	E

ANGEL
MANGER
MARY
JOSEPH
DONKEY
STAR
INN
STABLE

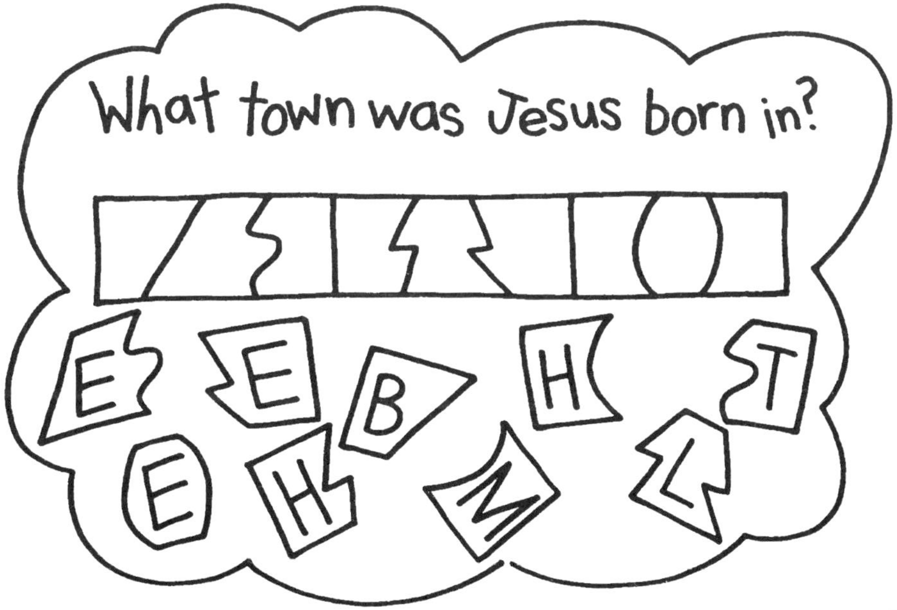

Colour this picture carefully.
As you do it, thank God
for coming into our world.

GOD IS WITH US.

Matthew 1:23

Colour this picture carefully, as a present to Jesus. Then you can give it to someone you love.

God let some shepherds share the secret. Most people thought shepherds were unclean but God loved them. Do you know what the angels sang to them?

3 6 8 9 12   11 8   3 8 1   5 7

11 4 2   4 5 3 4 2 10 11

D	E	G	H	I	L	N	O	R	S	T	Y
1	2	3	4	5	6	7	8	9	10	11	12

Luke 2:8-20

Which 2 angels are exactly the same?

Colour this picture of the shepherds on the hills above Bethlehem. WHAT HAPPENED NEXT?

Luke 2:9

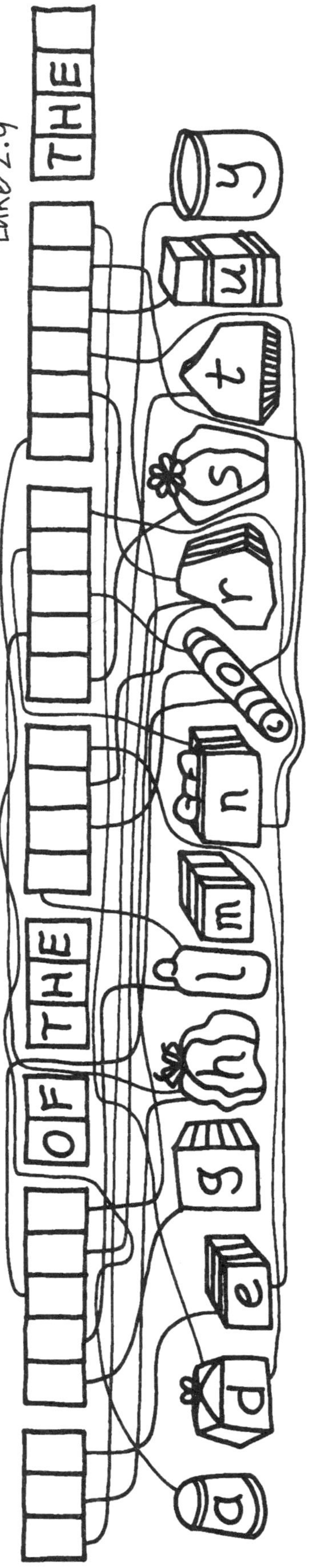

LED TO JESUS

Matthew 2:1-12

Can you help the wise men
to find JESUS?
Join the stars!

F	O	L	L	O	W	E	D	Q	J
A	P	B	C	F	I	E	D	R	E
H	D	R	G	E	S	S	I	M	S
X	L	A	E	M	E	N	P	Y	U
B	O	E	K	S	D	E	J	R	S
W	G	A	V	E	E	C	H	R	S
S	Z	G	C	L	T	N	O	H	U
Y	T	B	Y	F	X	I	T	V	T
Z	M	A	N	D	W	T	D	S	H
A	N	O	R	N	Q	G	C	K	E

THE WISE MEN
FOLLOWED A STAR
AND GAVE JESUS
PRESENTS: GOLD
INCENSE, MYRRH.

Stories with secrets

Jesus told stories
with secrets.
We call these stories:

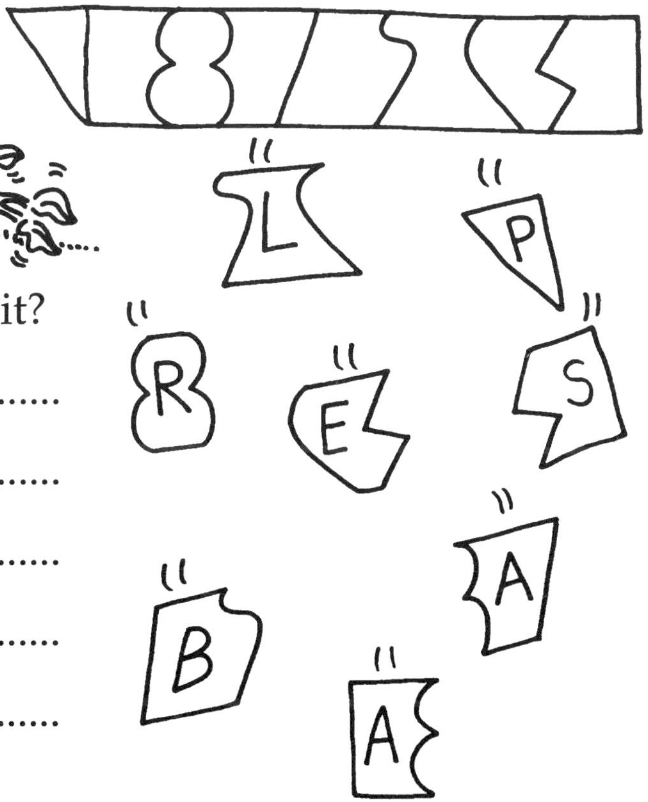

John 15:1-10

Which branch will not grow fruit?

Why not? ....

What's the secret meaning? ....

....

....

....

Matthew 18:12-14

What's the secret meaning?

....

....

....

....

....

....

....

If we are cut off from God we can't grow in love.

Jesus is like a good shepherd—if we get ourselves lost in life he will always come to find us.

JESUS DIED BECAUSE HE LOVES US

See Romans 5:8

Q. How can one grain of wheat feed millions of people?

See John 12:24

A. If you plant it, it will grow about 30 grains. Each of those grains can grow 30 grains and so on…

MATHS

1 grain grows 30 new grains

30 grains x 30 =	900 grains
900 grains x 30 =	27,000 grains
27,000 grains x 30 =	810,000 grains
810,000 grains x 30 =	24,300,000 grains

24 MILLION, 3 HUNDRED THOUSAND in just 5 years!

Colour this picture of Jesus on the cross. He must love us such a lot!

Jesus is risen from the dead

Stick this message inside card.

Fold

Jesus is alive for ever!

Jesus goes to heaven

Acts 1:9-11

Where do you live?

____

____

____

____

What school do you go to?

____

What church do you go to?

____

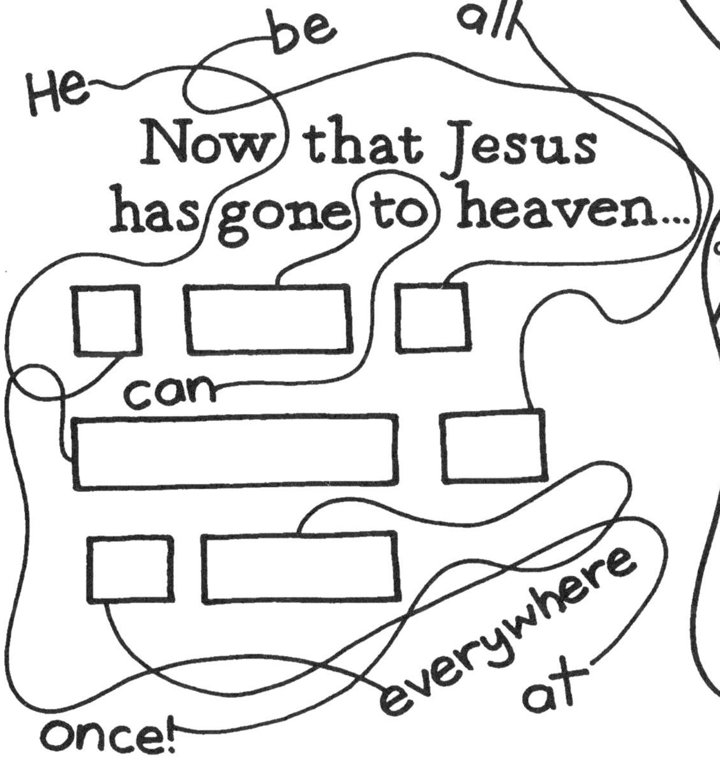

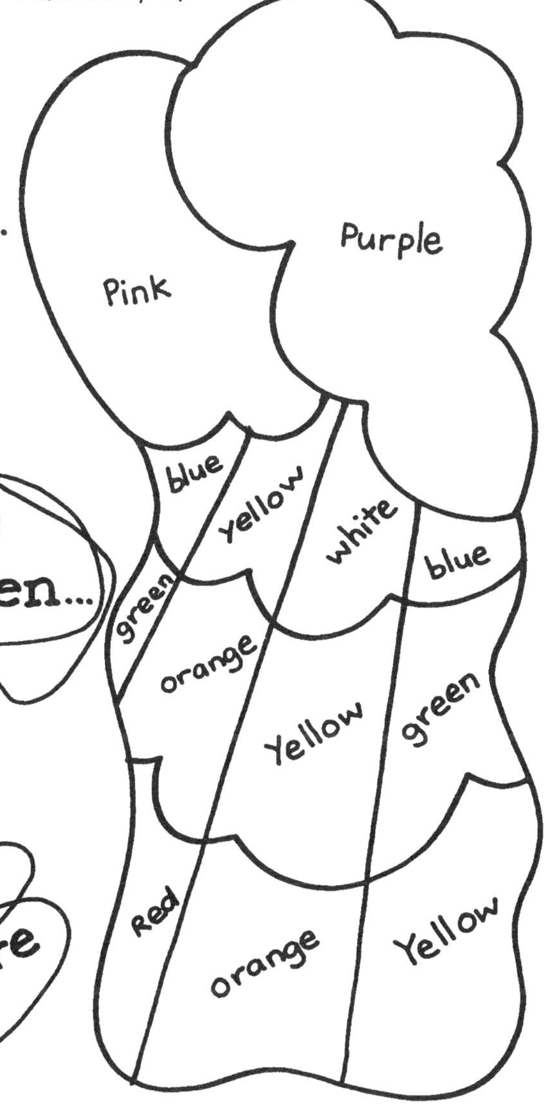

Jesus never leaves anyone out.

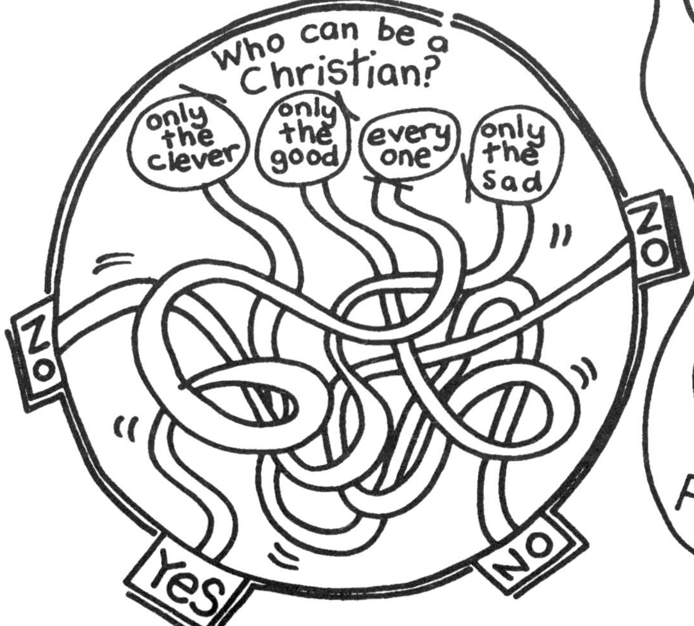

Sometimes we make people feel left out! Circle the things that do this...

What a weird haircut

I could go if I didn't have you to look after

Yes, I suppose you can come

Go away, we only have good players in our team

Come and join us if you like

How about you being referee! We need one

You want a drink, do you? But I've just finished washing up

Want a milkshake? –I'm just making one

Do come– I'm sure we'll all squeeze in

We haven't any room for you

Put a * next to the ones which make people feel welcome.

1 Draw lines round to separate the different groups of people.

2 Now draw a line God's way—it will include everyone.

God is real, even when we can't feel him there.

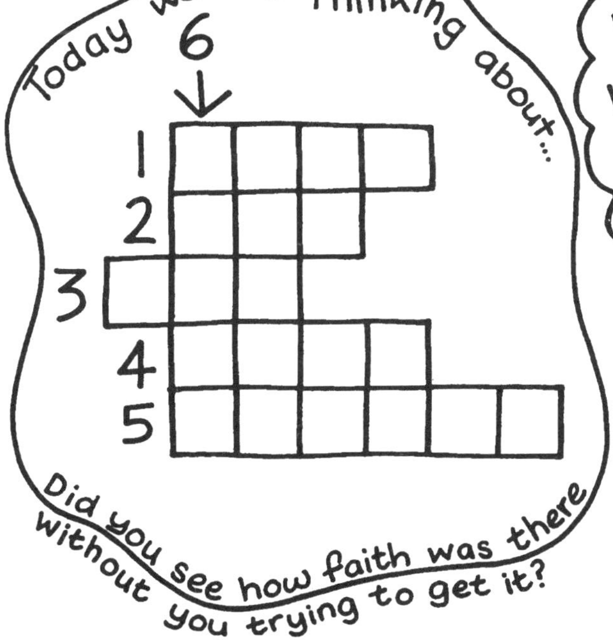

How can I know that God is real?

Here are some clues:

* Our lovely world
* The bible tells us
* Jesus was real in history
* When we pray he helps us

1. Where pigs and cows live.
2. Where Noah kept animals.
3. What makes God sad.
4. Another name for real.
5. Where God lives.
6. Trusting God and believing in him.

Can you see the wind in this picture? [ ]

Is the wind there? [ ]

GOD IS THERE, EVEN THOUGH WE CAN'T SEE HIM.

God always listens.

Draw what is under the water.

Draw what is under the ground.

G	I	X	T	O	W	T	J
G	O	A	H	J	Q	O	V
Y	N	D	B	B	K	O	T
T	C	F	I	U	M	S	I
O	U	L	I	S	T	E	N
Z	D	P	E	Y	L	R	G
N	E	V	E	R	B	E	U
D	O	C	A	F	H	I	S

GOD IS NEVER TOO BUSY TO LISTEN TO US.

God never forgets you–let him help you.

How good is your memory?

Shopping List

bread
4 yoghurts
tin of tomatoes
onions
crisps
jam

1. Read the list carefully.
2. Turn over and write them down or draw all you remember.
3. Check with the list.

HOW MANY DID YOU REMEMBER?

God's memory is

He doesn't forget

God knows that your name is

....

and that you live at

....

....

and that your best colour is

....

God knows you very well, and he loves you!

When we join Jesus he can help us, too.

Colour this picture of oxen yoked together.

We are safe in God's hands

DOT to DOT to see what is keeping Sam safe.

What are these things?—they all keep us safe.

ATES TEBL

EEMHLT

FILE AJKCTE

KLOC

But we are not just BODY.
We are SPIRIT as well.
What keeps our SPIRIT safe from evil?

Colour the picture

Learn to trust God

Here are some things that people trust more than God.

EOMNY

ODOG OLOKS

EIFTNSS

But we can't take any of these things with us past death.

When things go wrong

Life is not always easy, is it? We all have bad times and sad times.

How does God help?

God can...

| us | Help | brave. | to | be |

| us | Help | friends | again. | make |

| comfort | will | God | us. |

| keep | He | us | company. | will |

| us | forgive. | He | help | can | to |

Can you unjumble these?

How can we work with God?

We can [rebus] after 1 another,

4give 1 another and ♥ 1 another.

God or self? You choose!

1. Draw a car or a wedding.
2. Make it sunny or raining.
3. Colour it or leave it as it is.

Colour the good things the same colour as GOD
Colour the selfish things the same colour as SELF

You have just made three choices. God has made us able to choose.

How do you know what is right and what is wrong?

Listen to your:

Let your will be done

Matthew 6:10

You can choose GOOD.

You can choose EVIL.

Cross out the YES and NO words to read the message:

JYESESUSNODYESIDNONOTYESCHNOOOSE
TYESHENOEASYESYWANOY. HNOECHYESOSE
TNOHEGONOODWAYESYBECNOAUSEYES
HNOELOYESVESNOUS.

Lead us not into temptation.
Matthew 6:13

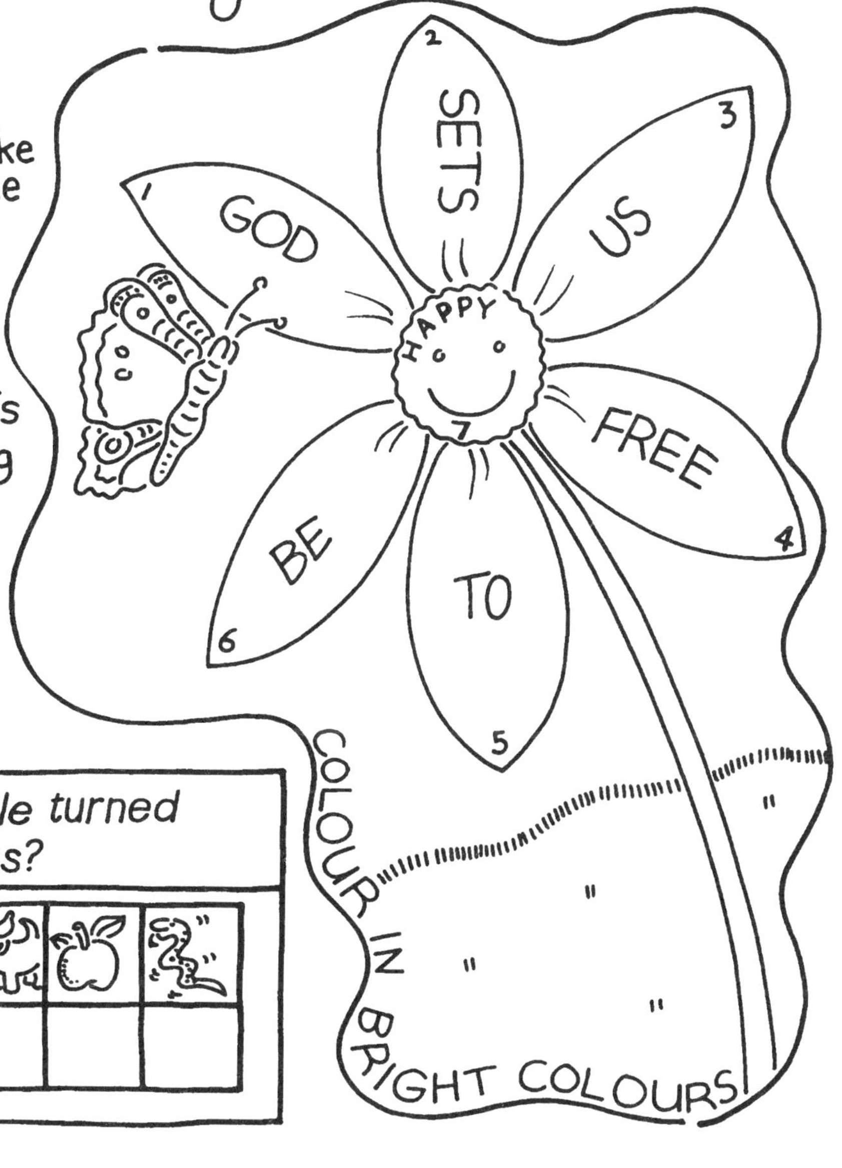

We are all tempted to grumble. Sometimes it gets to be a habit. But grumbling makes us, and those we are with,

Which disciple turned against Jesus?

What about the bad times?

We do not always feel ☺.
We all have ☹ times as well.

Think of the ☹ you have had

Colour this picture of fitness training.

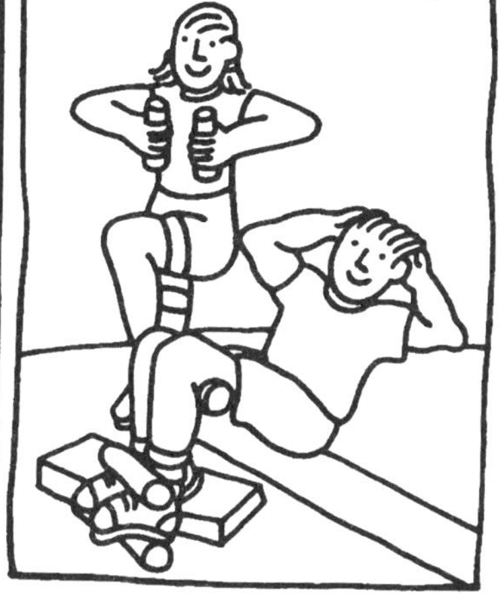

Sometimes the bad times can...

Here's what to do about them.

1. If it happened because you were being selfish
2. If it happened because someone was nasty to you
3. If it couldn't be helped, but was still sad

Tell God you are sorry. Let him forgive you and help put things right.

Forgive them!

Remember that it made God sad, too. He will help you cope with it, and bring good from it.

God puts things right.

There are 5 things wrong in this picture.
Can you spot them?

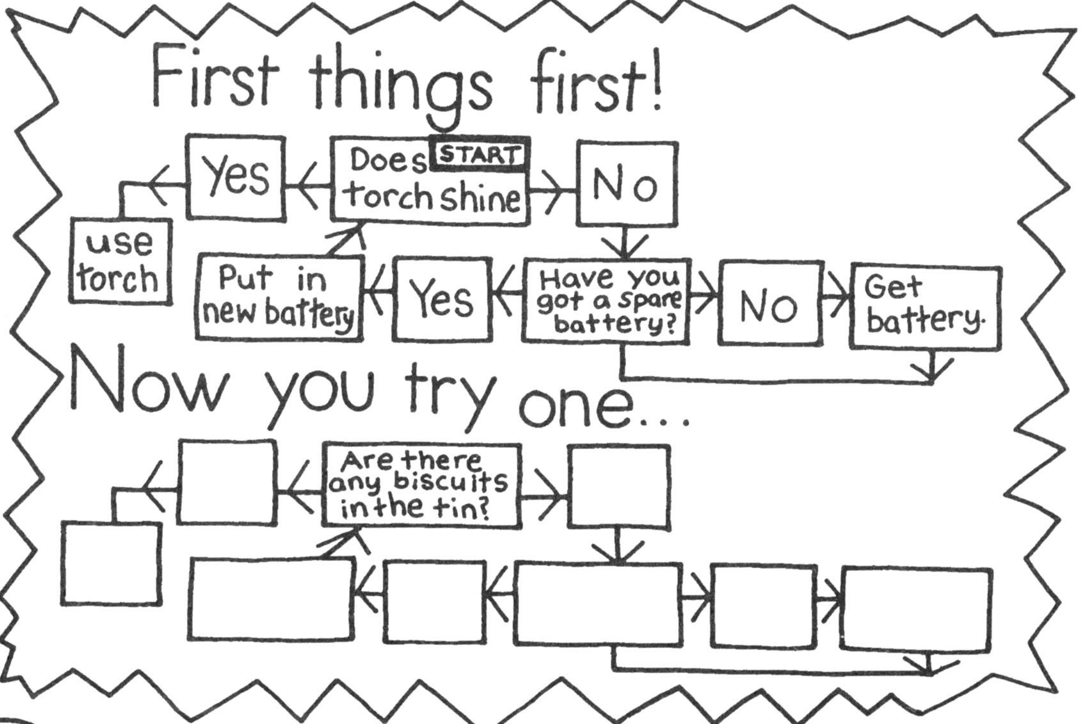

If w_ t_lk to God
_bout _v_rything th_t
go_s wrong, h_ will
h_lp us m_k_ it b_tt_r.

Help!
My typewriter can't type the letters e or a.

God is an expert at putting things right.
1. Write your friend's name at the bottom of this page.
2. Write another name on top of it.
3. Write your own name on top of that.
4. What a mess!
EXAMPLE
1. Eleanor
2. Ele
3. E
When we make a mess of things, God helps us sort it out.
STOP
SAY SORRY
PUT IT RIGHT
Colour the traffic lights
What to do when you SIN (act or think or speak in a way that makes GOD sad.)
scrape off paper
cut strip of paper
fill cracks in wall
paste paper
hang paper on wall
Put these instructions in order
1.
2.
3.
4.
5.
draw the pattern on the wallpaper
TE

Not patched up but made NEW!

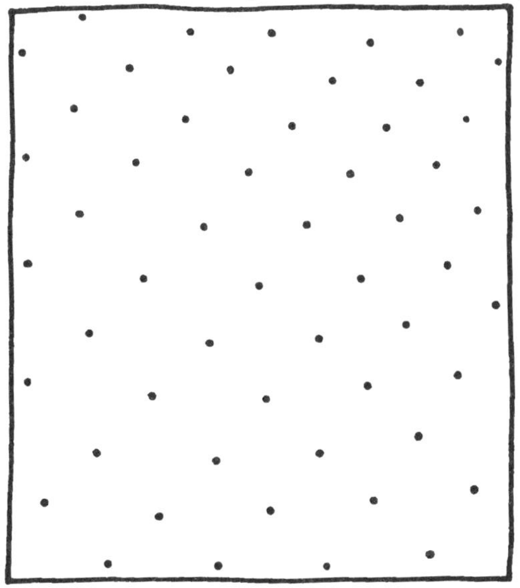

Make a new picture by joining up the dots how you like and colouring in.

Can you untangle the fishing lines—who has caught which fish?

Do you need God to sort you out in any of these things? Think it over, and talk to God about it.

BEING LAZY

Telling lies

SULKING

ARGUING

BEING A BAD LOSER

Being bossy

Sin destroys us... God can Save us

Colour in horrible colours

~ Colour in your favourite colours

L	H	A	B	T	R	U	S	T	C
O	F	E	H	E	I	K	D	L	J
V	N	G	L	M	E	R	C	Y	M
E	P	S	U	P	O	X	A	O	Z
B	V	E	G	T	O	H	T	U	J
T	Q	I	E	A	R	W	K	N	U
I	M	S	L	T	D	Q	Y	D	W
V	C	V	R	I	L	X	O	P	Y
Z	F	A	F	O	R	G	I	V	E
B	C	S	I	N	O	D	T	G	O

EVIL
SIN
LOVE
TRUST
HELP

TEMPTATION
MERCY
FORGIVE
GOD
YOU

Draw the reflections and colour the pictures.

REFLECT GOD'S LOVE

God sets people free.

Can you lead the person out of the maze?

Dot to Dot

If we spend our time being CORSS [ ] and RUGPMY [ ] look what happens→

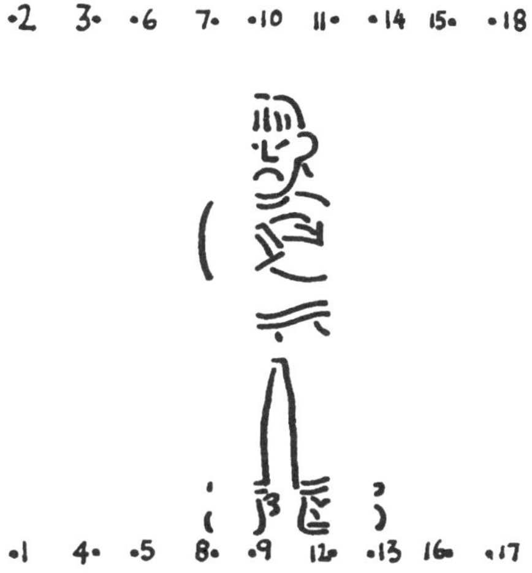

GOD CAN LET YOU OUT...

1. Tell God you are sorry
2. Ask him to help you put things right
3. Enjoy living again!

Being found when you're lost

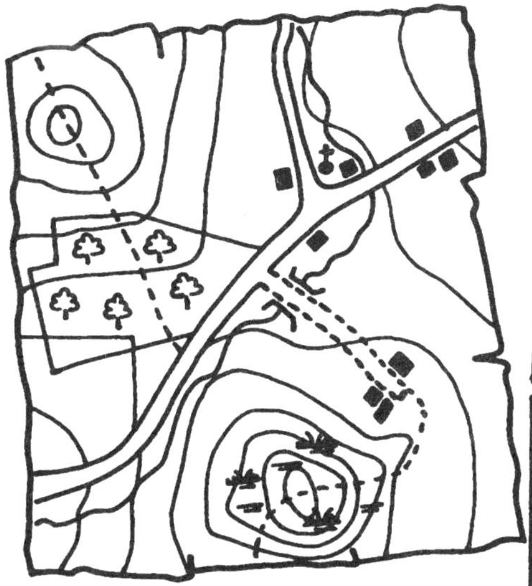

Can you find:

1. A church with a spire
2. A muddy hill
3. A wood
4. A bridge over a river
5. A steep footpath

Colour the picture

Draw a circle round the 'being lost' words. Draw a square round the 'being found' words.

sad
lonely
happy
worried
fed up
scared
thankful
relieved
pleased
excited

Being forgiven is a bit like being found

Draw in your face when someone says

I forgive you!

Q. How many times must we forgive someone?

A. _ _ _ _ _ _ _ _ _ _ _

E = M = T = V =
I = R = Y =

I will pour out my Spirit on all my people
Joel 2:28
Acts 2:17
If someone comes to you hoping to find God's love, would they find you full or half full or empty?
If you want to be filled with God's Spirit, this is what to do...
R=red
Y=yellow
O=orange
Which holds most?
Number them in order
When the Spirit came to the disciples it looked like this

All God's sons and daughters

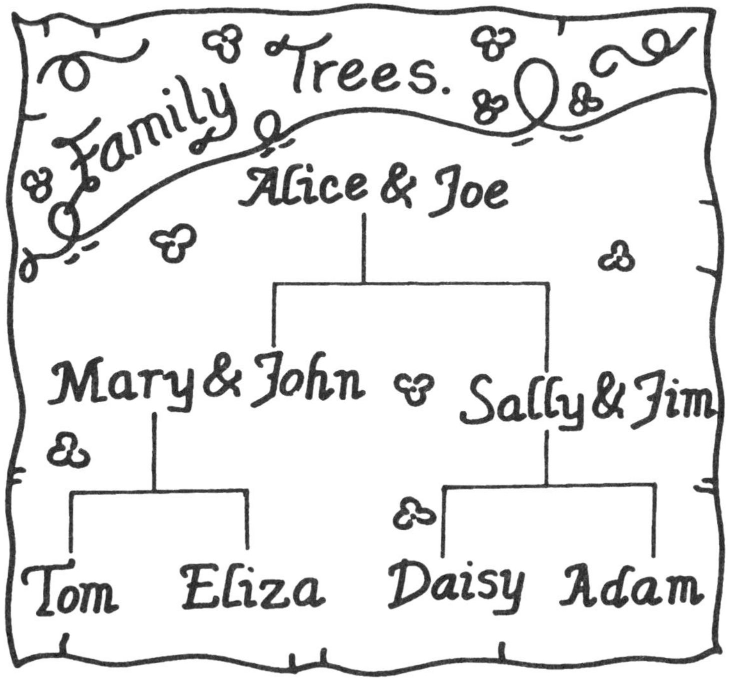

1. Adam's Dad is ______
2. Eliza's Mum is ______
3. Tom is Daisy's ______
4. Sally's brother is ______
5. Tom's auntie is ______
6. Alice and Joe have ______ grandchildren.

Look around at your brothers and sisters in God's family.
They are all loved by him.

Draw some of them here.

Love and respect each other.
If your enemy is thirsty...
pretend you have not noticed
give him a drink
give him an empty glass
Is there anyone new in church today? Make them feel
Colour this picture of some families coming in to church.

Helping one another along.

What things weigh people down?

Choose one from the list and write it in the weight.
- SADNESS
- MONEY WORRIES
- LONELINESS
- FAMILY ROWS

How could you help,
when someone falls over? ....
when Mum's in a hurry? ....

Love your enemies?

Matthew 5:44

HELP!!

Draw in something for this person to hang on to, so they won't fall down.

But enemies hate you ~ how can you love them?

But can give own need love strength

On your ☐☐☐ you can't. ☐☐☐ with God you ☐☐☐ because he will ☐☐☐☐ you the ☐☐☐☐ and ☐☐☐☐☐☐☐☐ you ☐☐☐☐.

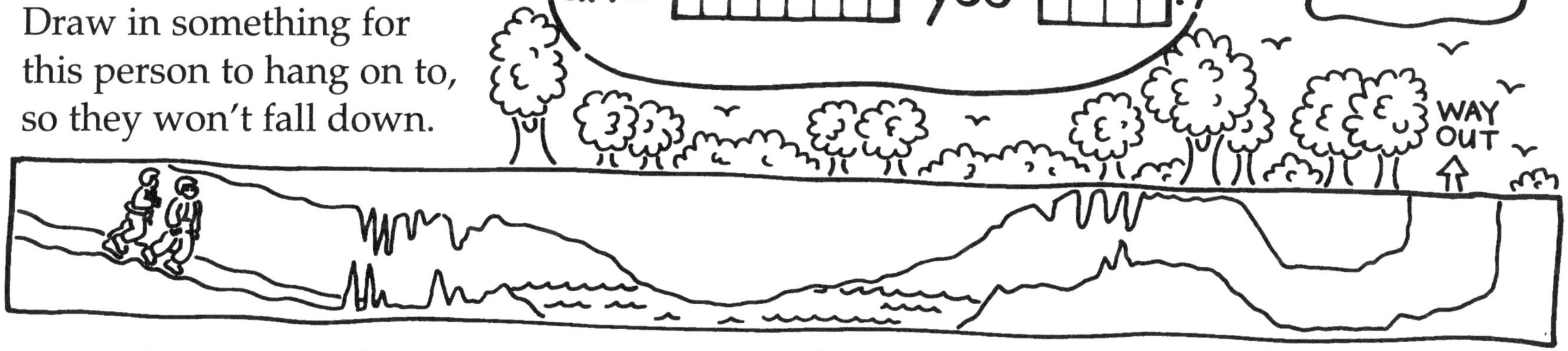

Draw some things to help these people find their way safely out of the cave.

Love your enemies

Matthew 5:44

Colour in the dotted shapes to see the message.

Draw a picture of you doing it.

✓The right way to behave
✗The wrong way to behave

Live to the full!

1) How many feet have you got? ☐

2) How many fingers? ☐

3) How many nails? ☐

4) How many hairs on your head? ☐

(Bet you couldn't do the last question!)

Some things we can do.
Some things we can't do,
and never will be able to.

What things do you like doing? Write them here and thank God for them.

....

....

....

....

....

....

....

....

....

....

....

....

Living as God wants us to live

Match the objects with the right jobs

- playing football
- doing the shopping
- ironing
- cleaning the house
- digging the garden

Think how hard it would be to play football with an iron, or clean the house with a shopping trolley!

Draw what happens to these things in time.

If we let Jesus take charge in our lives...

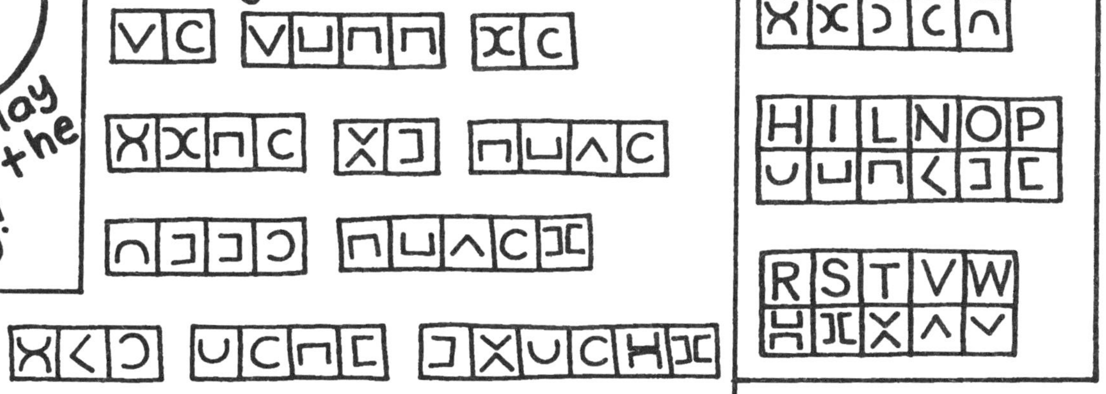

All set to get on with God's work.

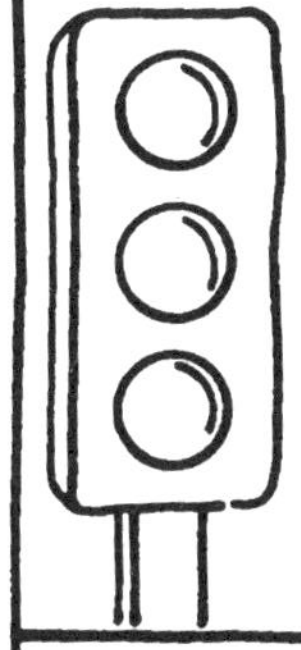

Colour the traffic lights so they say, 'GET READY TO GO.'

Draw in the runners in the 'GET READY' position.

Draw the children waiting to go on stage.

What do you need to do God's work?

to be grown up

to listen to God

to be ready

to be fit

to be a doctor

to pray

to have 'A' levels

to be happy to do whatever God suggests

to be able to swim

Circle the right ones, cross out the rest

HOW CAN YOU DO GOD'S WORK TODAY?

ideas

___

___

Is freedom doing what we want?

God holds us safe. He loves us so much.

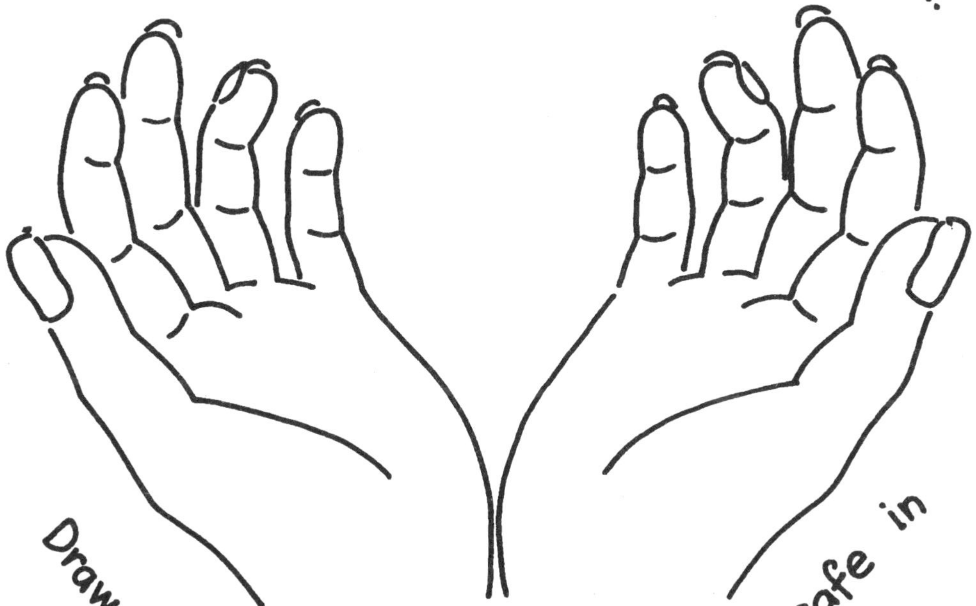

Draw yourself, your family and friends safe in the hands of God.

Jesus sets us free. Circle the things we can now do, and cross the things we aren't free to do.

forgive your enemy

laugh at people

enjoy yourself by hurting others

stop feeling guilty

be bossy

enjoy yourself

be happy, even when the car breaks down

STEAL

make people feel silly

True FREEDOM sets us free from

So that we are free to